שְׁמַע

The שְׁמַע expresses a feeling and a belief so strong it is unlike anything else—and so deeply felt that there are almost no words to describe it. This prayer is our pledge of loyalty to God; when we say it, we are expressing our belief in only one God who created the entire universe. The שְׁמַע expresses the very core of our faith. It is such an important and intense prayer that many people recite it with their eyes closed so they can concentrate completely on this pledge. The first line of the שְׁמַע declares our belief in one God; the second line praises God's name.

The first line of the שְׁמַע is said in a loud and clear voice.

שְׁמַע יִשְׂרָאֵל: יְיָ אֱלֹהֵינוּ, יְיָ אֶחָד.

Hear O Israel: Adonai is our God, Adonai is One.

These words come from the Book of Deuteronomy in the Bible. They became part of our prayer service about 2,000 years ago.

שְׁמַע
hear

יִשְׂרָאֵל
Israel

יְיָ
Adonai

אֱלֹהֵינוּ
our God

אֶחָד
one

WHAT'S MISSING?

Complete each prayer phrase with the missing English word.

שְׁמַע   _____ O Israel

אֶחָד   Adonai is _____

יִשְׂרָאֵל   Hear O _____

יְיָ   _____ is our God

UNSCRAMBLE THE PRAYER

Put the שְׁמַע in the correct order by numbering the words from 1 to 6.

יְיָ יִשְׂרָאֵל שְׁמַע אֶחָד אֱלֹהֵינוּ יְיָ

◯ ◯ ◯ ① ◯ ◯

Think About This!

In ancient times, Jews recited the שְׁמַע, declaring their belief in only one God—even while many other people believed in many gods, for example, a sun god, a moon god, a god of life, and others. It was not easy for the Jewish people to be true to their belief when everyone else felt otherwise. Have you ever been in a situation where your opinion was different from everyone else's but you stuck to it anyway? Why was it important to you?

Prayer Building Blocks

אֱלֹהֵינוּ "our God"

The word אֱלֹהֵינוּ is made up of two parts:

אֱלֹהֵי means "God of."

נוּ is an ending that means "us" or "our."

אֱלֹהֵינוּ means "our God."

Circle the Hebrew word that means "our God" in the following prayer:

שְׁמַע יִשְׂרָאֵל: יְיָ אֱלֹהֵינוּ, יְיָ אֶחָד.

Write the ending that means "us" or "our." _____ .

Write the Hebrew word that means "our God." _____ .

Because our ancestors were the first to know that God is the One God of all the world, we feel especially close to God—and so we say *our* God.

READING PRACTICE

Practice reading the following סִדּוּר phrases.

Circle the word אֱלֹהֵינוּ wherever it appears.

1. רְצֵה יְיָ אֱלֹהֵינוּ בְּעַמְּךָ יִשְׂרָאֵל.

2. בָּרֵךְ עָלֵינוּ, יְיָ אֱלֹהֵינוּ, אֶת הַשָּׁנָה הַזֹּאת.

3. אַהֲבָה רַבָּה אֲהַבְתָּנוּ, יְיָ אֱלֹהֵינוּ.

4. הַשְׁכִּיבֵנוּ יְיָ אֱלֹהֵינוּ לְשָׁלוֹם.

In each of the sentences above, the Hebrew word for Adonai also appears. Write the Hebrew word for Adonai. _____

THE RESPONSE

The line following the שְׁמַע is spoken quietly.

בָּרוּךְ שֵׁם כְּבוֹד מַלְכוּתוֹ לְעוֹלָם וָעֶד.

Blessed is the name of God's glorious kingdom forever and ever.

These words are not from the Bible. They were first recited in the ancient Temple in Jerusalem. They later became the *response*, or follow-up, to the first line of the שְׁמַע prayer.

Practice reading the שְׁמַע aloud.

1. שְׁמַע יִשְׂרָאֵל: יְיָ אֱלֹהֵינוּ, יְיָ אֶחָד.

2. בָּרוּךְ שֵׁם כְּבוֹד מַלְכוּתוֹ לְעוֹלָם וָעֶד.

DID YOU KNOW?

Many congregations say the second line of the שְׁמַע in a quiet voice. Why?

Our tradition tells us that during the time when the Roman Empire ruled the Land of Israel, it was forbidden to praise any kings other than the Roman emperors. Rome sent spies to the synagogues to listen to the prayers, so the Jews would whisper the words that praised God as Ruler forever and ever.

Can you think of another example of people who might have to whisper to protect themselves?

PRAYER DICTIONARY

בָּרוּךְ
blessed, praised

שֵׁם
name

כְּבוֹד
glory of

מַלְכוּתוֹ
God's kingdom

לְעוֹלָם וָעֶד
forever and ever

WHAT'S MISSING?

Complete each prayer phrase with the missing Hebrew word(s).

name   בָּרוּךְ _____ כְּבוֹד

forever and ever   מַלְכוּתוֹ _____ _____

blessed   _____ כְּבוֹד שֵׁם

God's kingdom   כְּבוֹד _____ לְעוֹלָם וָעֶד

WORD MATCH

Match the English word(s) to the Hebrew meaning.

A. forever and ever   בָּרוּךְ ( )

B. blessed   שֵׁם ( )

C. God's kingdom   כְּבוֹד ( )

D. name   מַלְכוּתוֹ ( )

E. glory of   לְעוֹלָם וָעֶד ( )

An Ethical Echo

Read these lines from Pirke Avot:

There are three crowns: the crown of Torah, the crown of priesthood, and the crown of royalty. But the crown of a good name—שֵׁם טוֹב— excels them all.

Think About This!

What does it mean to have a "good name"—שֵׁם טוֹב? What can you do to ensure your own good name?

Prayer Building Blocks

מַלְכוּתוֹ   "God's kingdom"

The word מַלְכוּתוֹ appears in the second line of the שְׁמַע.

The word מַלְכוּתוֹ is made up of two parts.

מַלְכוּת   means "kingdom."

וֹ   is an ending that means "his."

מַלְכוּתוֹ   means "His kingdom" or "God's kingdom."

As God is neither male nor female, we translate the word מַלְכוּתוֹ as "God's kingdom."

Circle the word that means "God's kingdom" in the following prayer:

בָּרוּךְ שֵׁם כְּבוֹד מַלְכוּתוֹ לְעוֹלָם וָעֶד.

Write the Hebrew word that means "God's kingdom." _____

ROOTS

מַלְכוּתוֹ is built on the root מלכ.

The root מלכ means "rule." The three letters מלכ tell us that "king" or "ruler" is part of a word's meaning.

Circle the three root letters in this word.

מַלְכוּתוֹ

Write the root. _____ _____ _____

What does the root mean? _____

Read these words aloud. Circle the three root letters in each word.

יִמְלֹךְ   מַלְכָּה   מַלְכוּת   מַלְכֵּנוּ   מֶלֶךְ

FLUENT READING

Practice reading the lines below.

1. שְׁמַע יִשְׂרָאֵל: יְיָ אֱלֹהֵינוּ, יְיָ אֶחָד.

2. בָּרוּךְ שֵׁם כְּבוֹד מַלְכוּתוֹ לְעוֹלָם וָעֶד.

3. הַלְלוּ, עַבְדֵי יְיָ, הַלְלוּ אֶת שֵׁם יְיָ.

4. וְהוּא אֶחָד, וְאֵין שֵׁנִי.

5. בַּיּוֹם הַהוּא יִהְיֶה יְיָ אֶחָד וּשְׁמוֹ אֶחָד.

6. לֹא תִשָּׂא אֶת שֵׁם יְהֹוָה אֱלֹהֶיךָ לַשָּׁוְא.

7. צוּר יִשְׂרָאֵל, קוּמָה בְּעֶזְרַת יִשְׂרָאֵל.

8. שְׁמַע! בַּיָּמִים הָהֵם בַּזְּמַן הַזֶּה.

9. וְטוֹב וְיָפֶה הַדָּבָר הַזֶּה עָלֵינוּ לְעוֹלָם וָעֶד.

10. אַהֲבָה רַבָּה אֲהַבְתָּנוּ, יְיָ אֱלֹהֵינוּ.

11. וַיְהִי עֶרֶב וַיְהִי בֹקֶר, יוֹם אֶחָד.

Artist: Ilene Winn-Lederer; Photograph: Creative Image. ISBN 0-87441-755-4 (Sh'ma); Manufactured in the United States of America.